THE CIVIL WAR AND RECONSTRUCTION

CONTRA COSTA COUNTY LIBRARY

By Stuart Kallen

ABDO
& Daughters

Visit us at
www.abdopub.com

Published by ABDO Publishing Company, 4940 Viking Drive, Edina, MN 55435.
Copyright © 2001 by Abdo Consulting Group, Inc. International copyrights reserved
in all countries. No part of this book may be reproduced in any form without
written permission from the publisher.

Printed in the United States.

Edited by: Paul Joseph
Graphic Design: City Desktop Productions

Cover Photos: Corbis
Interior Photos: Corbis

Library of Congress Cataloging-in-Publication Data

Kallen, Stuart A., 1955-
    The Civil War and Reconstruction / Stuart Kallen
        p. cm. -- (Black History)
    Includes index.
    ISBN 1-57765-469-2
    1. United States--History--Civil War, 1861-1865--Afro-
Americans--Juvenile literature. 2. Afro-Americans--History--
1863-1877--Juvenile literature. 3. Afro-Americans--Social
conditions--19th century--Juvenile literature. 4. Antislavery
movements--United States--History--19th century--Juvenile
literature. 5. Reconstruction--Juvenile literature. [1. Afro-
Americans--History. 2. Antislavery movements. 3. Abolitionists.
4. Reconstruction.] I. Title

E540.N3 .K27 2001
973.7'415--dc21   00-056886

CONTENTS

Captain
John Brown
is captured
with slaves.

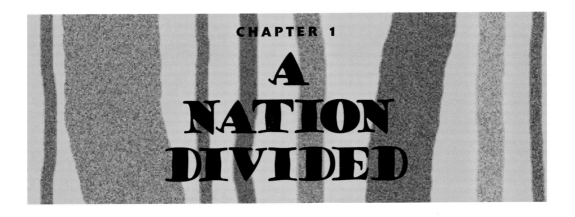

CHAPTER 1
A NATION DIVIDED

In 1808, the United States outlawed the international trading of slaves. But although the new law made it illegal to import slaves, the government did not enforce this law. The coast of the southern United States was left unguarded, and slave smugglers took advantage. Up until the Civil War, American sailors continued kidnapping blacks in Africa and selling them in this country.

Slave
Auction

THE AUCTION SALE. Page 174.

Although importing slaves was made illegal in 1808, the number of slaves in the United States continued to grow. That year, about one million slaves lived in the United States. Washington, D.C., was the heart of the slave market. Slave caravans and auctions were common in the nation's capital and in other southern cities. When the Civil War began, over four million slaves lived in this country. Slavery had been a part of America for over 240 years.

American laws considered slaves to be a special kind of property. There were different laws for whites and blacks. Slaves could not own property, be legally married, strike a white person, or possess guns. In Mississippi, no slave was allowed to beat a drum or blow a horn. The Constitution said that all people were created equal, but this idea was not applied to slaves and free blacks.

Free Blacks

Denied Most Rights

In 1860, around 500,000 free blacks lived in America. Nearly half of them lived in the South. But many states made it difficult for these people to make a living. In Maryland, blacks needed a special license to sell corn, tobacco, or wheat. Once black people left a state, they were not allowed to re-enter. They were not allowed in restaurants or on public transportation. In many states, blacks were also denied the right to vote. In 1840, Maine, Massachusetts, New Hampshire, and Vermont became the first states to grant full voting rights to black men.

In many places, it was illegal to teach blacks to read and write. Many states, however, had secret underground schools. In large cities, free blacks organized clubs and societies to aid each other. They opened schools, churches, and businesses. Blacks became doctors, lawyers, carpenters, and shopkeepers. Some also moved to the new western territories, because they did not like the racist attitudes in the East.

African-American
school children

New States and Slavery

Dividing Congress and the Country

In 1803, the Louisiana Purchase nearly doubled the size of the
United States. By 1850, all of the land from Mexico to Canada and
from the Atlantic Ocean to the Pacific would become part of
America. Each time another territory became a state, Congress
had to decide whether slavery would be legal in the new state. By
1820, 11 states approved of slavery and 11 were against it. This
meant that in any vote about slavery, the Senate would be evenly
divided.

In 1818, Missouri wanted to join the United States. Angry
debates took place in Congress over whether slavery should be legal
in Missouri. These debates went on for months. In January of 1820,
Maine was admitted as a free state. At this time, the northern and

southern senators reached an agreement. Maine would become a free state and Missouri would become a slave state. This would maintain the balance of power in Congress.

When they did this, Congress also drew an imaginary line across the United States. Slavery would be illegal in new states north of the line. South of the line, slavery would be legal in any new states. This act was called the Missouri Compromise.

By 1850, California, New Mexico, and Utah all wanted to become states. Most northerners did not want slavery in the new states, but most southerners did. For nine months, bitter debates raged in Congress. Some southern states threatened to secede. Finally, the two sides reached a compromise. This compromise had four points. First, Congress would admit California as a free state. Second, slavery would be legal in New Mexico and Utah. Third, the slave trade in Washington, D.C., would end. Fourth, Congress would protect slave owners by passing strict fugitive slave laws.

This Compromise of 1850 was not a long-term solution to the differences between North and South. The southern states discussed leaving the United States and forming their own country. Many northerners did not want slavery in the new territories. And the fugitive slave laws upset blacks and northerners.

Henry Clay, an American Senator who engineered the Compromise of 1850 which sought to avoid civil war.

The Fugitive Slave Law

The fugitive slave laws of 1850 made it the government's job to catch runaway slaves. Federal officers received payment every time they returned a runaway slave to his owners. There were stiff penalties for anyone who refused to help these officers.

Catching runaway slaves became a profitable business. Many escaped slaves were sent back to their plantations, where they were whipped, beaten, or even killed as punishment for running away.

In many cases, the men who were searching for runaway slaves did not care if they caught a free black or a runaway. They were only concerned with earning money. Many free blacks were kidnapped and sent to face a life of slavery. They could not protest, because blacks were not allowed to testify in court.

Nat Turner's Rebellion

Bloody Revolt Ends With Stricter Laws

Nat Turner was a slave in Southhampton County, Virginia. He was a religious man who preached on Sundays and was respected by both whites and blacks. People called him "the Prophet." But Turner felt that his life was useless as a slave. He wanted to free the black race from the chains of slavery. As he worked in the fields, he looked heavenward for a sign from God. In February 1831, there was an eclipse of the sun. Turner thought the eclipse was the sign he had waited for. He gathered his friends and planned a massive slave uprising for the Fourth of July. But Turner became ill and had to cancel the plans.

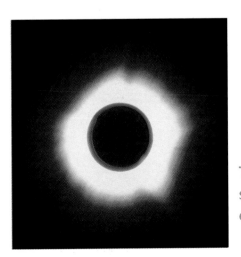

Total solar eclipse

A wood engraving depicting the discovery of Nat Turner, an African-American slave who led the Southampton Insurrection in August of 1831.

On August 13, Turner saw another sign: a greenish-blue haze covered the sun. Once again, he planned an uprising. The uprising began with Turner and six other men. On August 21, 1831, they killed Turner's owner, Joseph Travis, and Travis's wife and children. Two other people were also killed. Eventually, Turner's force grew to around 75 slaves. They killed around 60 people during their rampage.

News of the revolt soon reached the local sheriff, and hundreds of men picked up their guns and went searching for Turner and his men. When they found the rebels, dozens of slaves were killed. Turner avoided the police for two months, but was finally captured by the Virginia militia on October 30, 1831. He was put on trial and found guilty. On November 11, Turner was hanged.

At his trial, Turner said that the sun would refuse to shine on the day he was hanged. He said it would be a sign from God that slavery was evil. Many people scoffed at Turner's prediction. But the local sheriff took him seriously. The sheriff refused to cut the rope that would drop Turner to his death. No one else in the county would do it either, so an old tramp who lived 40 miles away was brought in to be the executioner. On the day of the hanging, a huge thunderstorm darkened the sky with black clouds. Many people thought that this was the sign that Turner had predicted.

Turner's Rebellion touched off a wave of violence against blacks. Seventeen men who had fought with Turner were hanged. Many slaves who had nothing to do with Turner were also killed. Slaveholders organized militias in case another rebellion started. Strict laws were passed to tighten owners' control over their slaves. Slaves were no longer allowed to assemble, even for church services.

The Abolitionist Movement

People who wanted to end slavery were called abolitionists. After the Revolutionary War, free blacks became more and more opposed to slavery. Many taught themselves to read and write. These black abolitionists spoke and wrote about the evils of slavery. White abolitionists joined them and toured the country demanding freedom for the slaves. Abolitionists wrote, prayed, and preached a message of freedom.

Abolitionist and newspaper publisher William Garrison.

Many people disliked abolitionists. One was killed by a mob in Illinois in 1837. Many southern post offices refused to deliver antislavery newspapers. The state of Georgia offered a $5,000 reward to anyone who brought William Garrison, a famous abolitionist, to trial. Many white people were worried that if the slaves were freed, blacks and whites would be competing for the same jobs. These people booed and harassed abolitionists wherever they spoke.

The Underground Railroad

Songs and Stars Led Slaves to Freedom

The Underground Railroad was not underground, nor was it a railroad. It was a network of black and white people who helped slaves escape to freedom in the North. Thousands of people, both black and white, risked their safety to help runaways escape. After the fugitive slave laws were passed, runaways were no longer safe in the North. Many went to Canada in order to be free.

People who helped runaways on the Underground Railroad were called conductors. These conductors led slaves along back roads in the dead of night. During the day, slaves hid in barns, basements, or attics. Officials hunted them with bloodhounds. Places where slaves hid were called depots or stations. Conductors provided runaways with food and clothing. Night after night, they continued on their difficult journey toward freedom. Levi Coffin, a Quaker, was called "President of the Underground Railroad." He assisted more than 3,000 slaves.

A slave needed courage and skill to run away. One man nailed himself in a box and was mailed to the North. Another walked 1,500 miles in shoes he carved out of wood. Slaves passed along secret information in song lyrics. The song "Follow the Drinking Gourd" referred to the stars that formed the Little Dipper. That constellation included the North Star. Runaways used it to direct them to the North. The gospel song "Swing Low Sweet Chariot,

Henry "Box" Brown rises out of a shipping crate amid men from the Underground Railroad.
He shipped himself out of the South to escape from slavery.

Coming for to Carry Me Home" meant that a person from the Underground Railroad was "coming for to carry" a slave home to freedom. The song "Wade in the Water" told runaways to travel in rivers and streams so that dogs could not track them.

Many Underground Railroad conductors were sent to jail, and some were murdered. But slaves continued to escape on the Railroad until the Civil War. Scholars estimate that around 75,000 slaves rode the Underground Railroad to freedom.

Uncle Tom's Cabin

The Evils of Slavery Reach Thousands

Harriet Beecher Stowe was a white abolitionist from Cincinnati, Ohio. One day she heard about Eliza, a slave who decided to run away to Canada in the middle of the winter. Eliza and her baby escaped from a farm in Kentucky. They journeyed north to the Ohio River. The river was only partially frozen, and so Eliza and her baby could not cross. They waited through the cold winter night for the river to freeze.

The next morning, Eliza saw slave catchers and bloodhounds coming for her. She wrapped her baby around her in a shawl and jumped. From one iceberg to the next, Eliza made her way across the icy, flowing water. In time, Eliza reached Canada. The following summer, she returned to Kentucky and helped her other children escape to freedom.

Harriet Beecher Stowe decided to write a book about slavery and include Eliza's heroic journey. Stowe titled the book *Uncle Tom's Cabin*. It was first published in a magazine in 1851, one chapter at a time. *Uncle Tom's Cabin* became an instant best seller. No book had ever sold so fast. Over 300,000 copies were sold in the first year. The book was sold in England, France, and Germany, but it was banned in the South.

American author Harriet Beecher Stowe

Uncle Tom's Cabin was based, in part, on the life of a slave named Josiah Henson. In the story, Henson describes how an angry slave owner cut off his father's ear. After Stowe's book became a best-seller, she received an envelope from the South. When she opened it, out fell a slave's ear—a threat from a plantation owner.

Uncle Tom's Cabin helped many people see the evils of slavery. More and more people became abolitionists, and the nation became more deeply divided.

Poster advertising *Uncle Tom's Cabin* by Harriet Beecher Stowe

The Dred Scott Decision

Pushing the Country Closer to War

Dred Scott was born a slave in Virginia around 1795. His owner died in 1831, and he was sold to John Emerson, an Army surgeon. Emerson and Scott spent three years in Illinois, a free state, and two years in Wisconsin, a free territory. In 1839, Emerson and Scott returned to Missouri.

When Dr. Emerson died in 1843, Scott tried to purchase his family's freedom from Emerson's wife. When Mrs. Emerson refused, Scott's abolitionist friends told him to sue. They argued that he should be free, because of the years he spent in free territory.

Scott lost his case, but he appealed the decision. He won the second time, but the Missouri Supreme Court overturned this ruling in 1852. With the help of white abolitionists, Scott took his case to the U.S. Supreme Court.

The Chief Justice of the Supreme Court, Roger B. Taney, was a southerner who approved of slavery. On March 6, 1857, the Court decided that because Scott was black, he was not a citizen of the United States. Therefore he had no right to sue anyone. The Court also said that Congress could not prevent slave owners from taking their property, including slaves, anywhere in the country. In his decision, Taney wrote, "Blacks are an inferior class of being and have no rights which the

Chief Justice of the Missouri Supreme Court, Roger Brooke Taney

white man is bound to respect." Only two of the nine Justices opposed this ruling.

In the South, the Court's decision was widely celebrated. But Taney's racist statements enraged many northerners. Protest meetings were held throughout the country. The Dred Scott decision brought our nation much closer to war. People no longer felt that a peaceful solution to slavery was possible.

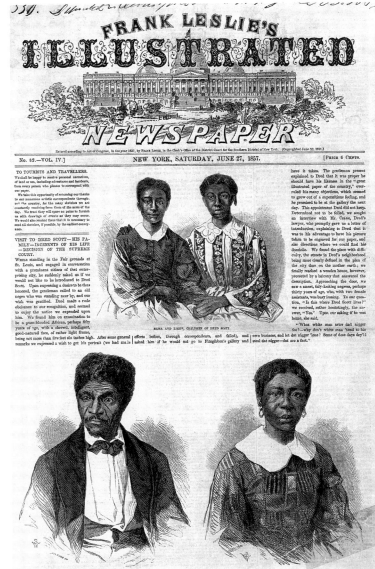

A copy of Frank Leslie's Illustrated Newspaper has a front page story on the Supreme Court's anti-abolitionist Dred Scott Decision of 1857. The story includes illustrations of Dred Scott and his family.

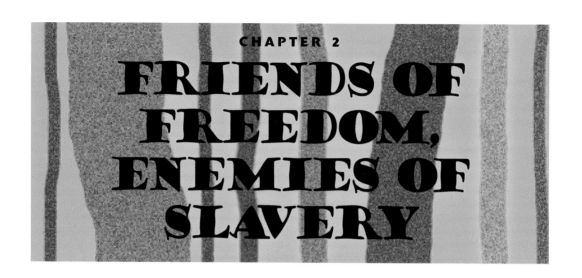

CHAPTER 2

FRIENDS OF FREEDOM, ENEMIES OF SLAVERY

John Copeland, Jr. (1836–1859)

Fighter for Freedom

There is a famous song that goes, "John Brown's body lies a-mouldering in the grave but his truth goes marching on." John Brown was a white abolitionist from Kansas. Brown was convinced that slavery should be ended immediately. He planned to lead a slave revolt in Virginia.

John Copeland served time in jail for helping a runaway slave. When he was released, he joined up with John Brown.

The Abolitionist John Brown

A view overlooking Harpers Ferry and the Shenandoah River in West Virginia during the Civil War.

On October 16, 1859, Brown, Copeland, and 21 other men captured an armory and arsenal in Harpers Ferry, West Virginia. An alarm was sounded and soon the Virginia Militia and the U.S. Marines, led by Robert E. Lee, surrounded the fighters. Dangerfield Newby, a free black who hoped to free his slave wife and children, was the first to die. Brown's two sons were shot next.

Colonel Robert E. Lee

Soon eight more men lay dead. One man, a college student named Osborn Anderson, managed to escape. John Copeland, John Brown, and five others were captured. After a long trial, they were sentenced to death.

On the evening before he was to die, Copeland wrote a letter to his brother. "I am not terrified by the gallows," he said. "I am soon to stand and suffer death for doing what George Washington was made a hero for doing. I am dying for freedom. I could not die for a better cause." On December 16, 1859, Copeland was hanged for fighting for the freedom of slaves. The execution of Copeland and John Brown's men angered abolitionists all over the country. It was one of the final acts that touched off the Civil War.

Frederick Douglass (1817–1895)

Influential Publisher, Speaker

Frederick Douglass was born in Maryland in 1817 and named Frederick Bailey. His mother was a slave, and he did not know his father, who was white. When Douglass was a boy, his mother was sold to a plantation 12 miles away. Sometimes after work, she would walk that long distance to see her son. When Douglass awoke in the morning, his mother would be headed back to the plantation for another day of labor. She died when Frederick was about seven years old.

As a child, Douglass's only clothing was a rough, knee-length shirt. In the winter, he used a burlap sack as a blanket while he slept on the floor. Often he wrestled with "Old Nep," the dog, for scraps of food that had been thrown out.

Later Douglass was sent to Baltimore, Maryland. There he learned to read and write. When he was 16, Douglass refused the orders of his master and was hired out to Mr. Covey, a well-known "slave breaker." Covey constantly beat and whipped

Douglass, until one day Douglass resisted. He parried Covey's blows for two hours, until both men were exhausted. Covey never beat him again.

Later, Douglass planned an escape. He and five other men would steal a boat and row 70 miles across Chesapeake Bay. Then they would hike into Pennsylvania. Douglass forged "free papers," but he was arrested before the plan could be carried out.

Douglass was sent back to Baltimore to work in the shipyards. There he fell in love with a free black woman named Anna Murray. Murray and Douglass plotted another escape attempt. By borrowing free papers from a black sailor, Douglass was able to escape to New York City. Douglass sent for Anna and they were married. The day after the wedding, they sailed to New Bedford, Massachusetts. To avoid slave hunters, Frederick changed his last name from Bailey to Douglass.

In Massachusetts, Douglass met William Lloyd Garrison, publisher of an antislavery newspaper. Garrison introduced Douglass to abolitionists who wanted his help. Soon, Douglass was asked to speak at rallies. He spoke so well that many people did not believe he had ever been a slave. To ease any doubts about his life, Douglass wrote a book called *Narrative of the Life of Frederick Douglass* in 1845. The book talked about slaves and owners, and about the places where Douglass had lived. The book was so detailed that Douglass was afraid his old owner would find him and come after him. He and his wife soon moved to England.

In England, Douglass lectured about slavery, women's rights, and world peace. His regal appearance and intelligent lectures won him many friends. Although his friends wanted him to stay in England, Douglass felt he should return to America to help end slavery. Douglass's English friends purchased his freedom, so that he would not be recaptured in America.

Frederick Douglass, a former slave, was one of the most important and eloquent advocates of abolition before and during the Civil War. After the war he served in several government posts, the first African-American to do so, and spoke and wrote frequently on civil rights issues for all Americans.

In 1847, Douglass settled in Rochester, New York. He started a newspaper called the *North Star*, in which he wrote of the evils of slavery. Douglass called for equal rights for Native Americans and women. When John Brown was arrested for raiding the Virginia arsenal, the Governor of Virginia accused Douglass of helping to plan the raid. Douglass was forced to flee to Canada.

When the Civil War started in 1861, Douglass urged President Lincoln to free all the slaves and allow them to join the army. Shortly afterward, Lincoln issued the Emancipation Proclamation, which did what Douglass asked. Douglass also helped to recruit two all-black regiments in Massachusetts. His two sons were the first men to enlist.

After the war, Douglass was appointed to several important government posts. He was the marshal of the District of Columbia, recorder of deeds, and diplomat to Haiti and the Dominican Republic. After retiring, Douglass focused on solving the problems facing southern blacks. On February 20, 1895, he died of a heart attack.

Frederick Douglass was a great writer, diplomat, and speaker. He advanced the cause of freedom and liberty for blacks and whites alike. He is remembered today as the greatest black leader of the 1800s.

Harriet Tubman (1821–1913)

Conductor of the Underground Railroad

Harriet Tubman was perhaps the most famous conductor on the Underground Railroad. Slave owners offered a reward of $40,000 to anyone who captured her, dead or alive. Her philosophy is summed up in her quote, "You'll be free or die. There is two things I have a right to, liberty or death. If I could not have one, I would have the other. For no man shall take me alive." No one ever did capture Tubman. In all, she made 19 dangerous trips to the South. She brought over 300 slaves to freedom, including her own parents. Tubman never lost one slave in her journeys.

Tubman was born in 1821, in Dorchester County, Maryland. She was a highly intelligent child in a family of 11 children. Tubman was not allowed to learn to read and write. She spent her childhood working the fields. When she was a teenager, she tried to protect another slave who was being beaten. Her master threw a rock at her and the blow almost killed her. For the rest of her 92 years, Tubman suffered seizures and blackouts from that incident. Soon after, she began to hear voices and see visions warning her of danger and telling her to escape.

When Tubman was 28, she followed the north star to freedom in Philadelphia. Soon she joined the Underground Railroad and made

Harriet Tubman, herself an escaped slave, helped hundreds of slaves escape the South by means of the Underground Railroad.

her first journey to help runaway slaves. Between rescue missions, she worked as a cook and laundry washer to earn money. When she earned enough for another mission, she would disguise herself and head south into slave territory.

When Tubman passed white people in her disguise, they saw a half-crazed, harmless old woman singing gospel songs. They did not know that the songs were sung in code to alert slaves of her arrival. Slaves who joined Tubman had to follow her strict rules: Be on time, keep your plan a secret, follow all orders, and be prepared to die before turning back. Tubman carried a gun and threatened to shoot anyone who turned back. No one ever did.

During the Civil War, Tubman worked as a cook, nurse, scout, and spy for the Union Army. Some historians have called her the Union's best spy. On one raid, she helped to free over 750 slaves. After the war, Tubman organized schools for black children and spoke for women's rights. When she died in 1913, she was buried in Ohio with military honors. Flags flew at half-mast. Blacks and whites gathered to pay tribute to the brave conductor on the Underground Railroad. In 1978, the U.S. Postal Service issued a stamp honoring Tubman.

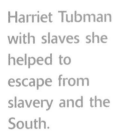

Harriet Tubman with slaves she helped to escape from slavery and the South.

Sojourner Truth (1797–1883)

Abolitionist, Preacher, Women's Rights Activist

Sojourner Truth was born in Hurley, New York, in 1797. Her name then was Isabella Baumfree. She was a slave, and she suffered terrible cruelties. Most of her 13 children were sold into slavery. Truth was sold four times. She finally ran away in 1826, one year before slavery was officially ended in New York. A Quaker family helped her win a lawsuit to have one of her children returned to her. When he was five, the child had been sold to a slave owner in Alabama.

Sojourner Truth was born into slavery but later freed. She worked as an abolitionist, a suffragette, and an evangelist and traveled throughout the Midwest drawing large crowds. She supported herself by selling copies of her book, *The Narrative of Sojourner Truth.*

Truth worked in New York and attended several churches. In 1843, a voice from God told her to change her name to Sojourner. The voice also told her to travel "up and down the land showing people their sins." Sojourner asked God for a second name. He told her to name herself "Truth," because she was to tell everyone the truth about slavery.

For 20 years, Truth traveled around the country speaking about slavery and women's rights. She had a deep, booming voice, and her speeches won the respect of many abolitionists. She was even invited to the White House to meet with Abraham Lincoln. During the Civil War, Truth raised money for black Union soldiers by lecturing and singing. Although she could not read, she became so famous that books were written about her. After the Civil War, Truth tried to obtain land in the West for newly freed slaves.

CHAPTER 3

THE CIVIL WAR

Abraham Lincoln

Policies Fueled the Fears Leading to War

In the 1850s, there were many great disagreements between the North and South. When Abraham Lincoln was elected President in 1860, the rift turned to war. Lincoln was a member of the new Republican Party. Republicans were against the expansion of slavery into any new states. Lincoln supported his party's position on slavery. But he also said that he would not free the slaves.

Abraham Lincoln, the 16th president of the United States, issued the Emancipation Proclamation abolishing slavery in 1863.

He promised to enforce the Fugitive Slave Law and allow slavery to continue where it already existed.

The southerners did not believe Lincoln. They decided to leave the Union, or secede, in order to protect their right to own slaves. On December 20, 1860, South Carolina became the first state to secede. By February 1861, Mississippi, Georgia, Florida, Texas, Louisiana, and Alabama had also seceded.

On February 4, 1861, representatives of the seven seceded states met in Montgomery, Alabama. They named their new country the Confederate States of America. On April 12, Confederate soldiers attacked Fort Sumter in South Carolina. This was the beginning of the Civil War.

Fort Sumter under the Confederate flag during the Civil War.

Blacks Not Allowed

The Civil War quickly turned into a bloody nightmare for both sides. New weapons killed hundreds of thousands of soldiers. There were few medicines to heal the wounded. Blacks, however, were ready to do battle for freedom and the Union. "Men of color, to arm!" wrote Frederick Douglass. Free blacks and slaves rushed to join the Union Army. Free blacks in Boston and New York formed all-black regiments at their own expense. Slaves left plantations by the thousands to help the cause.

But the Union did not want blacks to fight. The War Department was afraid that whites would not fight alongside black troops. President Lincoln said, "If I could save the Union without freeing any slaves, I would do it; and if I could save it by freeing all the slaves I would do it; and if I could save it by freeing some and leaving others alone I would also do that." Lincoln did not want to anger border states that were fighting for the Union. During the early days of the war, Union soldiers were instructed to return runaway slaves to their owners.

The Emancipation Proclamation

On January 1, 1863, Lincoln signed the Emancipation Proclamation. The Emancipation Proclamation declared that all slaves in the Confederate States were free.

The proclamation did not apply to the 800,000 slaves who lived in the Union. Maryland, Delaware, Kentucky, and Missouri were called the Border States. These were slave states that fought for the Union. Lincoln did not free the slaves in these states, because he was afraid they would become angry and join the Confederacy. Once, someone said to Lincoln that God would be on the Union side if he freed all the slaves. Lincoln replied, "We would like to have God on our side, but we must have Kentucky."

The Emancipation Proclamation also did not apply to parts of the South that had already been captured by Union troops. Thus it left many blacks still in slavery. However, the Emancipation Proclamation was an important step toward ending slavery in America. Slaves started running away in record numbers. Finally, the federal government supported freedom for all people, regardless of their race.

In 1865, Congress passed the Thirteenth Amendment to the Constitution. This amendment made slavery illegal everywhere in America. After 250 years of slavery, all Americans were finally free.

Black Soldiers in the Civil War

During the first year of the Civil War, blacks were not allowed to fight. They could only help white soldiers behind the lines. Blacks worked as horse drivers, cooks, blacksmiths, construction workers, and waiters. Frederick Douglass urged President Lincoln to allow blacks to become soldiers. Douglass said, "This is no time to fight

Men of Company E of the 4th United States Colored Troops stand outside their barracks at Fort Lincoln.

with only your white hand and allow your black hand to remain tied."

After the Union lost several important battles, many northerners realized that they needed the help of black troops. In July 1862, Congress passed a bill allowing black men to fight. After the Emancipation Proclamation, black men signed up for the Union Army in huge numbers. By the end of 1863, over 50,000 black soldiers were fighting in the Civil War. In all, over 200,000 blacks fought for the Union. Another 200,000 black men and women worked as scouts, nurses, guides, spies, cooks, and laborers.

African-American sailors aboard the *USS Vermont*. The United States Navy employed thousands of freed slaves during the Civil War.

The Life of a Black Soldier

Even during the war, blacks faced unfair treatment. White soldiers in the Union Army received 13 dollars a month, plus clothing expenses. But black soldiers received only 10 dollars. Black soldiers often received faulty equipment and poor medical care. A worse fate awaited black soldiers who were captured by the Confederates. Some captured soldiers were sold into slavery. Others were murdered. In 1864, over 200 black soldiers were massacred after they surrendered at Fort Pillow, Tennessee.

Lincoln issued an order stating that for every black prisoner killed, a Confederate prisoner would be killed. And for every black soldier sold into slavery, a Confederate prisoner would be subjected to forced labor. Blacks fought fiercely, willing to die before surrendering.

By the end of the war, 20 black soldiers had received the nation's highest honor, The Congressional Medal of Honor. But blacks paid a high price in the Civil War. Roughly 68,000 were killed or wounded.

After four bloody years, the Civil War finally ended on April 9, 1865. The North had won the war to end slavery and preserve the Union. But the whole country had paid a heavy price. It is estimated that 360,000 northerners and 135,000 southerners died during the war. The South lay

Taylor, the drummer boy of the 78th United States Colored Infantry Regiment, poses proudly with his drum.

Ex-slave children freed by Lincoln's Emancipation Proclamation line up outdoors at Freedmen's Village, a temporary settlement at Alexandria, Virginia.

in ruins. Millions of southerners were homeless and starving. And millions of blacks with no job skills or homes were suddenly free. Many of these people could not read or write. The freed blacks looked to the United States government for help.

Reconstruction

New Rights—Temporarily

In 1865, the federal government set up the Freedman's Bureau. The Bureau found homes and jobs for former slaves, provided them with medicine and health care, and protected them from unfair labor practices. The bureau built over 4,000 schools for blacks. Most southern whites were strongly opposed to the Freedman's Bureau. They still resisted equality for black people.

White politicians in the South passed "Black Codes." These codes prevented blacks from voting, getting jobs, and using public areas. To counter this, Congress passed the Reconstruction Act of 1867. The Act put 10 southern states under military law. Congress also passed the Fourteenth and Fifteenth Amendments to the Constitution. The Fourteenth Amendment guaranteed equal rights for people of all races. The Fifteenth Amendment guaranteed black men the right to vote. Other civil rights acts made it illegal to keep blacks out of hotels, theaters, railroads, and other public places.

The new rights mobilized large numbers of southern blacks to vote. Many blacks were elected to state and federal governments. Mississippi sent three black men to Congress. South Carolina sent two. Twenty-two black men served in Congress before 1900. Blacks were also elected as governors and judges.

The black legislatures enacted new laws that guaranteed free education for blacks. Other laws abolished criminal punishments like branding and whipping. Many civil rights laws of the 1800s are still in effect today.

In 1877, Reconstruction officially ended. The last federal troops left the South. Once again, southern blacks were left to fend for themselves. Even during Reconstruction, many blacks had been killed by white terrorists. Homes, schools, and farms were burned. Afterward, the problem became even worse. Southern states passed "Jim Crow" laws. These laws prevented blacks from using public transportation, theaters, and restaurants. They also made it extremely hard for blacks to vote or participate in politics. By 1901, there were no blacks in Congress.

TIMELINE

1808 United States outlaws the international trading of slaves

1820 Congress adopts the Missouri Compromise

1831 Nat Turner's Rebellion

1840 Maine, Massachusetts, New Hampshire, and Vermont become the first states to grant full voting rights to black men

1850 Fugitive Slave Laws passed as part of the Compromise of 1850

1851 Harriet Beecher Stowe's *Uncle Tom's Cabin* is published

1857 U.S. Supreme Court renders the Dred Scott decision

1860 Abraham Lincoln elected president

——— South Carolina becomes the first state to secede

1861 Confederate States of America formed

——— Confederate soldiers attack Ft. Sumter; Civil War begins

1862 Congress passes a bill allowing black men to fight for the Union army

1863 Lincoln signs the Emancipation Proclamation

1865 Federal Government establishes the Freedman's Bureau

——— Civil War ends

——— Congress passes the 13th amendment banning slavery

1867 "Reconstruction" begins

1868 Congress passes the 14th amendment guaranteeing equal rights to people of all races

1870 Congress passes the 15th amendment guaranteeing black men the right to vote

1877 "Reconstruction" ends

REBUILDERS OF HOPE

Robert Smalls (1839–1915)

Civil War Hero, Congressman

One day, Roberts Smalls was a 23-year-old slave who was forced to serve in the Confederate Army. The next day, he became a famous war hero. On May 13, 1862, Smalls crept aboard the Planter, a Confederate ship that was anchored at Charleston, South Carolina. The Planter's crew had gone ashore for the night.

Robert Smalls seized the *CSS Planter* from Charleston, South Carolina, and delivered her to the United States Navy.

Smalls, his wife and children, and several other people sailed the ship into the open seas. They flew the Confederate flag so that the ship could safely pass Fort Sumter.

The soldiers that saw the Planter pass saw Smalls with a large straw hat pulled over his face. They thought he was the ship's captain. When Smalls reached Union waters, he hauled down the Confederate flag and hoisted a white truce flag. Then he turned the ship over to the Union Navy.

President Lincoln awarded Smalls a share of the prize money for the ship. Smalls was made a pilot in the Union Navy. On December 1, 1863, he became the captain of the Planter. He piloted the Planter until the war ended.

When Smalls retired from the Navy, he was elected to the South Carolina House of Representatives. Later he was elected to the U.S. Congress. While in office, Smalls worked to promote black education. White terrorists never intimidated him. In 1913, Smalls single-handedly stopped two black men from being lynched by a mob in South Carolina. He was 73 at the time.

Booker T. Washington (1856–1915)

Educator

In 1865, the Civil War ended. That same year, Booker T. Washington turned nine years old. Washington did not have time to play with the other children. He had to wake up at 4 a.m. to work in the salt mines in Malden, West Virginia. At night, after his 16-hour shift, Washington learned how to read.

In 1872, Washington left home to attend an agricultural college in Virginia. A white friend paid for his tuition. Washington did not have money to travel, so he walked across West Virginia to reach the school. Later, he graduated with honors and gave a speech at commencement.

In 1881, the state of Alabama decided to build a school in Tuskegee to train black teachers. Washington's college suggested that he be the dean of the new school. Washington was determined to make the new school a success. He bought an abandoned plantation and turned it

Booker T. Washington was the first head of the Tuskegee Institute in Alabama

into a campus. Students built classrooms, a chapel, and dormitories. They learned farming, carpentry, shoemaking, and printing.

Soon the Tuskegee Institute became the leading black school in the United States. By 1888, it had over 400 students. Washington's efforts to raise money for the school brought him in contact with America's top white businessmen. Washington decided to establish the National Negro Businessmen League, to help blacks who wanted to run their own companies. He also wrote *Up From Slavery*, a book about his life that became a best seller. Washington advised presidents Theodore Roosevelt and William Taft about political issues.

Booker T. Washington was a hard-working, self-made man. His contribution to black culture can still be felt today.

A Final Word

By 1880, the Civil War was over and blacks were free. But most southern blacks were as poorly off as when they were slaves. Low-paying jobs were usually the only ones open to black people. Land and supplies were expensive, and blacks were forced to go into debt to keep from starving. The Civil War freed blacks from slavery, but their lives were still filled with hardship. To relieve this hardship, men like Frederick Douglass and Booker T. Washington began the fight for civil rights in America. This fight would continue for over a century.

The issue of slavery divided the United States in the 1860s. The Confederate states were for slavery while the Union states were against it.

Union States in 1864

Confederate States in 1864

INTERNET SITES

The African-American Mosaic

http://lcweb.loc.gov/exhibits/african/afam001.html

> *This site details black history from the colonization of Liberia to Roosevelt's "new deal" in the 1930s. Browse through the pictures of historical people and documents, or see what the other links have to offer.*

African-American Odyssey—Library of Congress

http://lcweb2.loc.gov/ammem/aaohtml/

> *This Library of Congress site contains a history of blacks in America from slavery to civil rights. Check out pictures, links to other sites, and a collection of works by influential blacks in history.*

The Civil War, A History of its Key Battles

http://www.ecsu.ctstateu.edu/depts/edu/textbooks/civilwarbattles.html

> *Take a look at the major battlegrounds of the Civil War and see how the fights were won or lost.*

GLOSSARY

Abolitionists—People who believed that slavery should not be allowed.

Compromise of 1850—An attempt to solve the problem of which western territories becoming states could have slavery. Northerners wanted no new states to have legal slavery, and southerners wanted all new states to have it. As a result of this compromise, California became a free state, New Mexico and Utah became slave states, the slave trade was abolished in Washington D.C., and fugitive slave laws were put on the books to protect slave owners. Neither northerners nor southerners were very happy with this compromise and the country grew closer to war.

Confederate States of America—The name taken by the seven states that seceded from the Union. These states were South Carolina, Mississippi, Georgia, Florida, Texas, Louisiana, and Alabama.

Dred Scott Decision—This Supreme Court decision of 1857 ruled that slaves were not citizens of the United States and therefore had no rights. The court also ruled that slaves were the property of their owners and could be taken anywhere in the country as slaves. This decision pushed the country to the edge of civil war.

Emancipation Proclamation—Declaration signed by Abraham Lincoln in 1863 that freed all slaves in the confederate states.

Fifteenth Amendment—Amendment to the constitution that guaranteed black men the right to vote.

Fourteenth Amendment—Amendment to the Constitution that guaranteed equal rights for people of all races.

Freedman's Bureau—Government program started in 1865 that found jobs and homes for former slaves, provided them with medicine and health care, and protected them from unfair labor practices.

Fugitive Slave Laws—These laws were passed as part of the Compromise of 1850, and they made it the government's job to catch slaves that had runaway from their owners. Officers were paid for runaway slaves that they captured, which led to many free blacks being kidnapped and sent south so the officers would make more money.

Jim Crow Laws—A set of laws in the southern United States that called for blacks to have separate public facilities from whites. Public restrooms, restaurants, schools, and transportation were all designated for white or black use.

Missouri Compromise—Act passed by congress in 1820 to settle the disputes about which new states could have slavery. An imaginary line was drawn between the North and South with slavery being legal in all new states south of the line, and illegal in all new states north of the line.

Reconstruction—Shortly after the civil war, the Reconstruction Act of 1867 put southern states under military law to enforce the rights of the newly freed blacks. The 14th and 15th amendments to the Constitution were passed during Reconstruction, giving equal rights to all races, and guaranteeing black men the right to vote. Federal troops left the south in 1877 marking the end of Reconstruction. Many blacks were elected to public office during this period.

Slave Auction—Place where plantation owners gathered to view and purchase slaves just arriving from Africa.

Thirteenth Amendment—This amendment to the U.S. Constitution, passed in 1865, made slavery illegal everywhere in the United States.

Underground Railroad—A network of abolitionists, both black and white, who helped slaves escape to the North. "Conductors" on the railroad would lead slaves out of the South in the night, and hide them in safehouses during the day. It is estimated that 75,000 slaves made it to freedom on the underground railroad.

INDEX